How to Build and Manage Virtual Teams

Copyright Notice

Copyright © 2017 by Andere Development, LLC

All rights reserved. No part of this publication may be reproduced, distributed, or transmitted in any form or by any means, including photocopying, recording, or other electronic or mechanical methods, without the prior written permission of the publisher, except in the case of brief quotations embodied in critical reviews and certain other non-commercial uses permitted by copyright law. Permission requests should be submitted to the publisher in writing at one of the addresses below:

258 Beartooth Parkway
Suite 100-138
Dawsonville, GA
30534
United States of America

Contents

Preface 7

Chapter One: Setting Up Your Virtual Team 9

Chapter Two: Setting Up Your Virtual Team 15

Chapter Three: Virtual Team Meetings 21

Chapter Four: Communication 29

Chapter Five: Communication 37

Chapter Six: Building Trust 45

Chapter Seven: Cultural Issues 51

Chapter Eight: To Succeed With a Virtual Team 57

Chapter Nine: Dealing With Poor Team Players 63

Chapter Ten: Choosing the Right Tools 69

Closing Thoughts 77

Leadership and learning are indispensable to each other

John F. Kennedy

Preface

Virtual teams are growing in popularity since many companies continue to grow and expand in different areas. But sometimes learning to manage a team that we can't physically see every day can be difficult.

When we learn how to manage our local teams, as well as our virtual teams, we can form a group that works together to increase productivity and provides a new perspective on any project.

Management by objectives works if you first think through your objectives.

Peter Drucker

Chapter One: Setting Up Your Virtual Team

Part One

One of the key challenges in managing a virtual team is creating one in the first place. The manager must find employees that can work well under minimal supervision and can function with different types of technology. Don't let geographical differences hinder the team you want to create.

Choose Self-Motivated People with Initiative

One aspect of working on a virtual team is the ability to be self-motivated and self-disciplined enough to finish the job without someone looking over your shoulder. When building your virtual team, choose employees that show self-motivation characteristics, such as making goals and having strategies for completing assignments. If looking to utilize current employees, look for employees who have had a proven record for getting assignments done and sticking to what they want to accomplish. If hiring from outside the company, look at the person's resume and see what kind of success they have had and how they reached it.

Characteristics of a self-motivated person:

- They don't fear failure

- They have definite goals

- They make plans

- They are flexible when faced with a problem

Face to Face Meetings at First (Kick-off Meeting)

Even though virtual team members will be working apart from each other, it is important to start the team in the same location, usually through some type of 'kick-off' meeting. At this first meeting, members are introduced to each other and usually exchange contact information. The manager would then usually introduce the goals, assignments, and future projects for the group. This is the time where employees can ask questions, discuss availability, and plan for what they will be doing during the course of the upcoming projects.

If geography is a problem for gathering everyone together, try to find a central location that is a fair distance from everyone involved. In some cases, employees may need to be present by phone or video to be a part of the meeting. Setting up a one-time video meeting or conference may be the only way to get some face time between all participants. Having that initial face time is very important to the overall success of the team.

Diversity Will Add Value

Any manager wants a team of employees that can all work hard and accomplish their goals, but in the same instance a manager needs each employee to be different in their own way and utilize what they have to offer. Each employee is different and has a different set of skills that they excel at. They are able to provide different ideas and opinions that can be shared with others and create a new, unique perspective. When we bring a diverse group of employees together, they are not only able to use their diverse skills to complement each other, but they can ensure their part of the project is done to the best of their abilities, making the overall assignment a great success.

Benefits of a diverse work group:

- Various ideas and perspectives

- Each employee excels at their skill set

- Contributes to the group as a whole

Experienced with Technology

One of the most important aspects of a virtual team member is the need to be experienced with various types of technology. Team members will be in different locations, but will still need to keep in contact. Many ways employees accomplish this is to communicate by phone, email, fax, or even video phone. An employee must know how to operate different forms of technology in order to stay connected to other employees and management.

Assignments and projects are often sent by electronic files in a variety of programs and shared among the group to edit and sent along. If employees do not have a high level of knowledge when it comes to technology, they may not be able to function well on a team that relies so much on it. Current knowledge as well as keeping up-to-date with new and emerging technologies is required for today's teleworker.

Practical Illustration

Janet was getting ready to form a new virtual team in their large tri-county area. She had several employees she wanted to assign to the team, but was unsure how they would manage, and if they could handle the work load. She reviewed several of their files and looked into what they have accomplished while working in the company. She found one employee that was great with figuring numbers and another that worked best with customers and clients. They both had experience with the company computers and software, so Janet decided to add them both to the team. She knew they would work well together to help the whole team.

Coming together is the beginning. Keeping together is progress. But working together is success.

Henry Ford

Chapter Two: Setting Up Your Virtual Team

Part Two

When employees are happy and work together, they work harder to accomplish the job. When establishing your virtual team, it's more than just employee skills and abilities – you have to consider how they interact with each other and socialize in a group. Some of these things you may not know in the beginning, but some of them you learn along the way.

Personality Can Count as Much as Skills

Many people can master a certain skill set or become experts in many abilities, but their personality while they do it is what can set them apart. The same thing goes for a virtual team. An accounting team full of employees that can balance a budget is great, but if their personalities don't work together and they don't have personality in their assignments, the experience is not as productive and can even have negative effects. When choosing employees to join your team, look at their personality and how they present themselves. These traits will speak louder than their skills alone.

Avoid negative personality types:

- "Negative Ned/Nancy"
- The "Downer"
- The Gossiper
- The Antagonist

Rules of Engagement

The rules of engagement on any team are an important base to build on. With a virtual team, it can be a crucial part of the team plan. These rules include basic concepts of who to contact and who will be in contact with them. Some organizations have nicknamed it 'the phone tree', in which a chart or graph is created with employee names and channels in which they can use to contact someone else. This is important to establish with your virtual team members to let them know where they can go with any problems or concerns so they don't feel lost when they are in an area by themselves.

Examples:

- Who do the employees contact for help?
- Who do they work with on a regular basis?
- Who do they contact with a complaint?

Setting up Ground Rules

Ground rules are guidelines that help form appropriate group behavior. By setting up ground rules at the beginning of your team's formation, it will help stop some problems before they begin. Many ground rules start with employee behavior, such as how to treat each other and some sort of 'code of ethics' but also include basic rules about behavior at work, such as deadlines and basic workplace behaviors. Other areas for ground rules include project deliverables, such as following deadlines and procedures for presenting an assignment. One commonly overlooked set of ground rules are rules for employee work hours, including attendance policies, procedure for calling in sick, and rules for clocking in and out. Although there are many areas to cover when establishing these rules, the team will run smoother when everyone knows what they can and cannot do.

Examples:

- Email usage
- Contact procedure
- Project deliverables and deadlines
- Employee respect
- Employee acknowledgement
- Adhering to employee schedules

Icebreakers and Introductions

Icebreakers and introductions are very important tools to use at the kick-off meeting. Introductions are especially important since it allows employees to get to know each other before they begin working together and are required to communicate back and forth. Icebreakers are a fun way to get each employee to interact in the group. This is often done with a small game or involving everyone in a group activity. In these activities, employees share their name, job title or position, and some sort of fun fact, such as their favorite hobby or vacation spot. Icebreakers and introductions allow employees to relax with one another by talking about themselves and learning things about their fellow team members.

Example Icebreaker activities:

- Talk about favorite foods

- Group people by common job duties

- Compare hobbies

Practical Illustration

Alex was almost done completing his newest virtual team. He picked a great group of employees that he believed would make a great contribution, skill, and personality wise. When they had their kick off meeting, Alex said he wanted everyone to introduce themselves to each other and become comfortable with their new team members. He asked each person to introduce themselves and then tell everyone the best place they have visited on vacation.

Soon everyone was talking about different destination and laughing together. Lastly, before giving their assignments, Alex laid out the ground rules for the team, including the points of contact, rules regarding work property, dress code, and who to contact with a problem. When the meeting was over, Alex was confident his team would do a great job, even if they were far apart.

Treat employees like partners, and they act partners.

Fred Allen

Chapter Three: Virtual Team Meetings

Now that you have your virtual team assembled, the next step is to effectively hold virtual team meetings with all of them. Just because your employees aren't at a table in front of you doesn't mean you can't communicate with them and guide them during a project. As with a normal meeting, there will be the issue with setting a good time, ensuring everyone shows up and making sure you deliver all the right information. The key is learning tools that can help you run a successful meeting, in person or virtually!

Scheduling Will Always Be an Issue

Virtual teams have a harder time scheduling meetings because the employees are not in the same location. Some employees are in different time zones, others work different hours while the rest may be constantly traveling. One tip for managing the employees' time schedules is to keep a log or chart of an employee's location, working hours and where they could be assigned later. With this tool, you can determine prime times to hold virtual meetings that won't conflict with someone's schedule.

If different meetings need to be held, plan a schedule with the employees regarding a rotation of employees staying late or coming in earlier to cover meeting times. Many employees are happy to abide by a schedule in which they can give their opinions. Be sure to remind employees of any consequence that can occur for not sticking with the schedule or not participating in the meeting, such as written warnings and disciplinary actions on their employee record. Understand that employees may still be hard to schedule even with adjustments. So have an alternate solution handy in case an employee cannot attend group meetings. Be flexible with employees that attend meetings outside of their normal work hours, offer the next day off or maybe a half day.

Have a Clear Objective and Agenda

An agenda is very important to have in any meeting and is more so in a virtual meeting because it keeps everyone on the same track. Outline what you want to discuss and accomplish from the meeting and jot down ideas on how you can make them happen. Include specific topics that need to be reviewed and events that have happened with the team. Employees need to know there a clear objective to the meeting and that it is not a waste of their production time. Share your agenda with the rest of the team so they can be aware of the purpose of the meeting and what they can contribute.

Tips for sharing your agenda:

- Include it in a mass email so employees can read ahead of time.

- On video calls, have the agenda displayed at all times on the screen.

- For conference call meetings, read over the agenda first and allow employees to take notes.

Solicit Additional Topics in Advance

Soliciting ideas before the actual meeting is an important tool to use when creating your agenda for the meeting. Speak with your employees and ask if they have any additional topics they would like included in the meeting agenda. Sometimes after the employees are aware of the original agenda, ideas or topics are added to the plate, either by management or other employees. However, don't leave these new topics as a surprise for the other meeting attendees.

It is important to share these additional topics with employees before they 'arrive' at the meeting so that they can be prepared and don't feel as though they were blind-sided. When employees know of the meeting topics ahead of time, they are able to research the topic ahead of time and be able to make a meaningful contribution when they participate in the next meeting.

Discourage Just Being a Status Report

Status report type information can be sent through email or other electronic messages because it often does not include much of a response from employees. It is generally one-sided information that is meant to be informative, not discussed in depth. One of the problems of a virtual meeting is that the moderator will do most of the talking and presenting, leaving the other team members feeling as though they are only there to hear the latest status report. The same can go for employees that come to the meeting to share their information and then sit out for the rest of the time. Encourage employees to ask questions and take notes of the information given. Set aside time for employees to share ideas with one another and engage in conversation or debate about the meeting topics. These meeting are meant to be a time of learning and interaction, not just one-sided information sharing.

Practical Illustration

Polly is holding her first virtual team meeting. She had some trouble setting up a good time for everyone since many of her employees work in different time zones. She made sure she outlined the meeting agenda ahead of time and emailed it to all of the employees a week before the meeting. Polly received a few additional topics to discuss from some of the other employees. She made sure to share them with the rest of the team and requested their input on all of the presented topics.

When it came time for the meeting, the team met over video chat and Polly checked to make sure everyone had attended. She had each employee state their business and what they needed to share. Before they logged off, Polly encouraged everyone to take a few minutes to talk among each other and share ideas about what they learned at the meeting. She wanted to be sure each employee was actively participating instead of just remaining in the background.

The effectively communicate, we must all realize that we are all different in the way we perceive the world and use this understanding as a guide to our communication with others.

Anthony Robbins

Chapter Four: Communication

Part One

Effective communication is a key component to any successful business. It is especially important when managing a virtual team because not only do you deal with traditional communication problems with employees, but virtual teams can face more obstacles trying to keep in touch. Learning helpful tools and techniques for effective communication can take any virtual team a long way.

Early and Often

Early communication means not waiting for a problem to happen before addressing it. Check in with your employees on a regular basis, whether by phone, email, conference, etc. Don't let employees struggle through a problem over a long period of time. Don't wait for them contact you; reach out to them to offer help. Contact each employee often and follow up after any problems they have reported. Keeping in touch with each employee not only cuts down on large problems, but it shows your support in the employee and can boost their morale substantially.

Tips:

- Create a regular schedule to check in with employees
- Find what methods work best for each employee
- Keep track of small problems that arise early to prevent bigger ones later

Rules of Responsiveness

Communication is a two way street and can shut down when one side doesn't contribute or doesn't act on their responsibility. When outlining communication techniques with your virtual team, one aspect to cover is the rules of responsiveness. Determine which forms of response are appropriate in various situations. Do you need a response right away? Is it something they can reply to later? Will you need a short or long response? When sending communication to employees, let them know how soon they need reply and how soon you expect to hear from them. Employees need to understand that the communication you exchange with them is very important and that they need to respond in a timely manner.

Face to Face When Possible

Sometimes communication needs to be made in person or face to face. Communication over the phone or email can often be skewed because there is a loss of tone and body language. Although this can be hard with a virtual team, there are ways the manager and employees can work together. If distance is somewhat small, arrange a time for employees to meet either at your office or theirs. If distance is too great, the next best option is to use some sort of video message system, such as Skype. Although it does not replace in person meetings, it allows the manager and employees to talk 'face to face' and monitor their tone and body language signals. Sometimes long distance communication just can't deliver an effective message – so never underestimate the power of talking in person.

Choose the Best Tool

Every form of communication has an appropriate tool to use with it. Some information can be delivered by informal methods, such as email or telephone calls. Informal methods are great to use when a short or quick answer is needed rather than a longer response. Participants can share information quickly and then continue with their work. Other messages should be delivered more formally, such as face to face talks or even in a group meeting.

Formal methods are better used for in-depth messages and descriptions. The information is often lengthy and may require explanation or presentations. Formal methods also allow participants to ask questions or add their input. To choose the best tool, the manager should determine how urgent the message is, how quickly it needs to be received, and what kind of response they are looking for. Once they determine what is to be shared and what they need in response, they can then choose the best tool for the job.

Practical Illustration

Zach was communicating with his virtual team about upcoming projects and assignments. When he gave the original assignments, he spoke with every employee in person when he assigned them their project. He continued to speak with them by email and text messages when they had small questions or needed a deadline reminder. Zach made sure that when he sent an employee an update he let them know to reply back within 24 hours with any questions or concerns and to acknowledge that they have received the information. He knows that his employees know how to reach him when they need something and he can reach them when he needs.

Communication- the human connection – is the key to personal and career success.

Paul J. Meyer

Chapter Five: Communication

Part Two

Poor communication among employees and management has been shown to cause low employee morale and a decrease in productivity. Sometimes employees can feel unsure about approaching you or are not sure what to do when they have a problem. Encourage your employees to engage in two way communication and ask question when they receive new information. When they know who they can come to in a jam, they will feel more comfortable communicating their needs.

Be Honest and Clear

One of the pitfalls about team communication is that we try to hide information from each other. Managers will try to 'sugar coat' a problem within the company or employees won't mention how hard they are struggling with an assignment. When speaking with your employees, don't try to hide facts behind blurred words. If you have to deliver bad news, be upfront and let them know what is going on. If you need to change something they are doing or working on, be clear as to why and the effect it will have on them. When we try to hide facts or information, employees can become skeptical and will eventually lose their trust in you.

Tips:

- Remain honest, even if it is a negative aspect.
- Speak clearly and don't hide the fact behind 'sugar coated' words.
- Ensure the employee is clear about what they hear (Any questions?)

Stay in Constant Contact

Nothing can be more frustrating than trying to reach a manager that has fallen out of touch. Employees need to be able to reach you during regular business hours and should always have a source to contact outside those hours (i.e. on-call, second shift manager). It is especially hard for virtual team members since they cannot always physically contact you and will need some other way to speak to you when needed.

It is important for you to stay in constant contact with your team members and ensure them that you are there for them when they need you. Some examples include sending daily emails to check on progress, or making regular meetings to follow up with employees. Make a note of employees that need your assistance more often and be sure to check up on how they are doing over time. By staying in contact now, you are helping to prevent further problems later.

Don't Make Assumptions

We all know that old saying of what happens when we assume. A common problem in communication is assuming that we have delivered all of the information needed or assuming that the employees will not have any trouble with their work. These assumptions can cause us to leave our team members out to dry and cause them to feel as though you are not there to help them. The employees can begin to resent you and may feel too uncomfortable to ask for further information.

Ask for employees to follow up on any information they receive, especially if they have questions or concerns. Periodically check on each employee's productivity and ask if they are having any difficulties or need another problem addressed. Your team members can benefit from your guidance, so don't assume they will make it on their own without you.

Set Up Email Protocols

Email is one of the most important forms of communication on a virtual team. It allows a person to send a message from anywhere, and at any time. Unfortunately, it can often be misused and can lead to confusion and upset team members. When the virtual team is formed and introduced to using email, introduce employees to the rules and regulations of using email for contact purposes. Outline when it should be used in different situations and stress that is it for company business, not personal usage. Many companies require employees to sign a form acknowledging that they are aware of the email protocols and will abide by them. Again, don't assume your employees know the protocol and follow up with them to check for any questions.

Practical Illustration

Allison has been managing her virtual team for several months. She sends them information on a weekly basis and follows up with her team members regularly. Although she receives emails regularly, protocol states that any problems or concerns should be addressed another way, such as by phone or in person. One of her employees, Bob, has had some trouble earlier when he is supposed to format his end of the month reports. When she last spoke with him, she was upfront and clear about his poor performance and helped him outline ways to improve. The deadline was approaching, and Allison did want to assume that he was not having trouble again. She called his location and checked on his progress. Bob let her know that he was doing better and had fixed his previous errors. Even though he didn't need her help, Allison was sure to let him know that she was there for him if he needed her.

Learning to trust is one of life's most difficult tasks.

Isaac Watts

Chapter Six: Building Trust

Creating an open and honest environment in the workplace is a key factor to keeping employees happy and productive. On a virtual team, it is just as important to remain open with your team members and keep them in the immediate loop of information. Since they are not always in a central location, it is essential to keep them updated on current happenings in the company and in their department. When the employees feel included, they learn to trust you and will look to you when they have questions.

Trust Your Team and They Will Trust You

Trust is a key component in any relationship, personal or professional. Virtual teams can have additional problems with trust when they are not always in each other's company. They can be unsure about what is being said or if they are doing as well as they should. As a manager, it is important to show your trust in your employees first. Show them that you trust them to complete their work and trust them with crucial information, such as potential job reassignments or even closures. When the employees feel as though you trust them, they can, in turn, learn to trust you. They will instill their trust in you and confide in you when they have concerns or are worried. This trust not only builds a stronger relationship among the employee and manager, but also the entire virtual team.

Beware of "Us vs. Them" Territorial Issues

Often times when management tries to solely run a team without regards to its members, the employees can begin to have that "Us against Them" mentality. They begin to believe that management is only looking out for management or does not value the opinion of the team members. This can cause further resentment from employees and can affect the whole team's productivity. Remind your employees that you are on their side and that you realize that the team works together to accomplish the same goal. Let them know that they are included in many of the decisions made (although not ALL of them), and that their presence on the team is valued. When employees feel as though they are part of the working machine, they are less likely to feel like an opposing force.

Share Best Practices

A form of 'best practice' is loosely defined as a practice that has proved productive in the past and has results behind it to back it up. Sharing best practices with your virtual team can be a great move when faced with some of the same situations. Common forms of sharing these practices including sending them through email or forming some kind of instruction sheet. Some employees may need to be counseled in person or shown how to follow a process step by step. Sharing these practices shows trust among employees and trust that they can continue the chain of success.

Best practices:

- Processes/procedures that have worked before
- Can be shared a number of ways, including email, videos or personal instruction
- Consult with employees regarding alterations/variations if needed
- Follow up with employees to ensure comprehension

Create a Sense of Ownership

One overlooked method of building trust among your virtual team is helping them create a sense of ownership. Employees feel more passionate about their jobs when they feel as though they not only have a part in the team's success, but can feel as though their part is essential to the overall success. Although it can take a good amount of time to help an employee establish their sense of ownership, it can prove beneficial for everyone in the long run.

Tips:

- Ask what you can do to accomplish something
- Encourage every new idea
- Make a plan and put into action

Practical Illustration

Adam is a new manager and wants to build trust with his new employees. He decides to hold a meeting and meet them all personally. He introduced himself to each employee and told them about himself and what he would be doing as their manager. After all, he wanted them to trust him, not fear him. He assured them that he wanted to work with them, not above them, and wanted to see the team succeed. Once they started discussing the team's assignments, Adam opened up about some of his best practices that he used in the past and explained how he wanted to give them a test run with this team. He made sure they all felt as though they were a part of the planning process because he wanted them to feel like a team.

We can all do better when we work together. Our differences do matter, but our common humanity matters more.

Bill Clinton

Chapter Seven: Cultural Issues

Cultural issues in the workplace have been a hot topic for many years. They are more than just demographics and cannot always be detected right away. Even though team members may be from the same office or a similar location, each one has their own unique culture and following. It is important to embrace these differences and acknowledge the cultural issues that may be present. This can help the team build successful relationships with each other and prove more productive in the long run.

Respect and Embrace Differences

Diversity among a group is always a good thing, but under the wrong impressions it can ruin any team. Whether the difference is a type of culture, political opinions, or simply a difference in background, all these factors can change how a person interacts with another person and what kind of view they have. When team members are diverse, it can keep the team from thinking on one path and stop the 'one track mind'. It opens teammates up to new ideas and points of view, which in turn can create new concepts for projects and assignments. Together, they can learn to not only respect their differences among each other, but embrace them to create a whole new work style.

Be Aware of Different Work Styles

Sometimes different work styles on a team can be a good thing because they allow each employee to think on their own and work within a design that works best for them. Other times, it can be a real source of trouble if not properly addressed. Some employees may prefer to work alone even though they are needed on a team project. One employee may be a procrastinator and wait until the last minute to complete their assignment. The key is to learn to be flexible with one another and adjust how you approach each other. No two people work the same way, so any team, especially a virtual one, will need time to adjust to one another and learn what makes the other team member work so hard. When we know how they function, we can work in sync with them without a hitch...most of the time!

Know Your Team Members Cultural Background

On a virtual team, it can be hard to get to know your teammates personally since you are so limited in communication and socialization. Even if the members meet during some sort of meeting or conference, it can be hard to acknowledge a person's cultural background. Some companies have an employee fill out a personal profile that can be shared with other employees, which allows them to better know the person even though they are not in the same office. When we can better understand a person's cultural background, we can better understand why they do some of the things they do and can make them feel more comfortable on your team.

Examples:

- Provide an "All About Me" survey to gather information about employees

- Some information can remain private if desired, such as religion or political views

- Acknowledge cultural instances, such as holidays and rituals

Dealing with Stereotypes

Stereotypes can ruin any team relationship or bond. The sweeping generalization a stereotype can cause people to become confused or view people in a negative light, even if it was unprovoked. Knowledge and understanding are the only tools we can use to deal with stereotypes. Get to know your employees and encourage them to get to know their coworkers. Learn more about the employee as a whole person instead of what their cultural background may have been labeled as. Through observation and interaction, the chances of anyone creating or following stereotypes in the virtual team decreases and employees are able to focus on the task at hand, and not each other.

Practical Illustration

Cheryl is managing a virtual team that has offices all over the state. Because they are from different areas, Cheryl knows they all have different cultural backgrounds and different views and opinions. She decided to have every employee fill out a form of personal information they wanted to share with the rest of the team so that they can get to know each other better. She then decided to hold a video conference call where each team member could meet 'in person' and talk among each other. Here they discussed their profiles they finished and talk about their type of working styles and processes. Cheryl pointed out to the group that this is the time to demolish any stereotypes each person may have about someone else. She wanted the team to get to know each other and respect one another since they will be working so closely together.

All our dreams can come true if we have the courage to pursue them.

Walt Disney

Chapter Eight: To Succeed With a Virtual Team

Succeeding with traditional face-to-face teams can be challenging enough, but succeeding with a virtual team can be just as hard, if not more so. Inspiring a team to create and meet goals, maintain motivation and work together are only a few obstacles when managing a team that you cannot see on a daily basis. But with effective communication and a little discipline, any virtual team can succeed.

Set Clear Goals

Setting goals are one of the most elementary processes that can lead to success. After all, you don't know where you're going until you determine what you want! Clear goals are normally set for the team as a whole as well as each individual teammate. The manager works with the team to determine what they want to achieve over a set amount of time (i.e. increased sales, decreased absences) while the employee sets their own goals about what they want to achieve as a member of the team (i.e. decreased data errors, increased personal productivity). Setting goals with your virtual team can help them stay task-focused and can make them feel as though they are making a difference on the team.

Tips for setting goals:

- Determine what you want to achieve
- Define a path that can help you get there (there may be more than one)
- Decide what you will do when you reach that goal

Create Standard Operating Procedures (SOPs)

A Standard Operating System is generally a company's process or procedure that it follows in the workplace. Sometimes a company does not feel the need to document these procedures, since many people may already know it. But creating these procedures and correctly documenting them allows the manager to share them with other employees and create them as a type of guideline and resource. As a manager, review some of the procedure and processes that have worked for you in the past and try to create them into an SOP. Although it can be time consuming, it will be worth the benefits in the end. On a virtual team, these can be especially helpful for employees who may not have experience on the team yet. They will come to you for help and will need to learn procedures if they are to contribute to the team.

Build a Team Culture

Your virtual team is your family. Every member should take the time to know each other and familiarize themselves with someone else's situation. After all, every member of the team is a human being and deserves to be treated with respect and friendliness. If employees are not able to socialize locally, allow them to have a chat room on a private server or virtual community they can come and go in to speak with other employees on a non-business level. If possible, assign projects or assignments in pairs or small groups to encourage further mingling and socializing. When the employees feel as though they are part of a family, they see other teammates as family also and will create their own team culture they can fit into.

Provide Timely Feedback

Positive or negative, feedback is a great tool to help employees at work. On a virtual team, giving timely feedback is important to the team's overall success. Employees need to know how they are doing on assignments and need to know if they need to change anything. Since the manager cannot randomly approach the employee to give feedback as they would in person, it is best to set up regular, scheduled sessions (such as by phone or chat) to alert the employee of any negative feedback that needs to be addressed or any positive feedback that should be shared. This will require the manager to get to know the employee personally so that the feedback sessions are not awkward or uncomfortable.

Practical Illustration

Scott was re-evaluating his virtual team and looking over their recent progress. He has already implemented a timely feedback procedure which helps him deliver any tips or suggestions to his employees. But he wants the team to feel more like a family, so he decided to have a conference call with his team and check in to see how they were doing. While on the call, Scott mentioned that he wanted the team to feel closer together, and wanted to use this time to create clear and productive goals for the team and for each employee. He also wanted them to review some of their current SOPs and determine if any of them needed to be altered or changed, depending on whether or not they were working for everyone. Every employee contributed to the conversation and had some great ideas. By the end of the call, Scott had felt like his employees were closer now than before and would be able to work better together in the future, which would lead to more success for the team as a whole.

An employee's motivation is a direct sum of interactions with his or her manager.

Bob Nelson

Chapter Nine: Dealing With Poor Team Players

When we manage a team, there will always be a time where we have to address a member, or members, that are not working well with the group. No one wants to be the bad guy, but if the employee is not confronted and not given the chance to improve, it can affect the other members of the team and could cause a 'domino effect' for productivity. Learn the techniques of approaching this delicate situation and lookout for your team as a whole – not just one member.

Manage Their Results, Not Their Activities

When a person manages an office, they can see for themselves what an employee is doing or what they are working on. However, on a virtual team, the progress can be much harder to monitor. Because of this, it is more important to monitor the employee's results, rather than the individual activities. If the employee is delivering great work and it's on time, then the process of how they finish it means very little.

For many employees, having this sense of freedom and trust can boost their confidence and improve productivity. However, if an employee is not completing work on time or is not turning in projects, then this is an indication of poor work habits and the manager should investigate into what is causing the problem. Approach the employee and talk to them about their routine schedule. If needed, organize some form of an improvement plan to help them adjust their ways of completing their assignments.

Be Proactive, Not Reactive

It is better to be prepared for any mishap before it happens, which is why it is important to be proactive rather than reactive. If we wait for something to go wrong before we act on it, we cannot think clearly about what to do and it may be too late to fix. The same theory goes for team members. Do not sit back and wait for them to make a mistake before they are taught how to do something correctly. Monitor each employee's progress and notice any minor problems they may have along the way. Speak to the employee early on when they problem starts and try to find a way to guide them on the right path. This will prevent the problem from getting worse and having to use more damage control later. Being proactive will always keep you one step ahead and ready to help the employee succeed.

Check In Often

On the same lines of being proactive, be sure to check in with your employees often. They may not always have the chance to contact you or may not want to admit they need help. Schedule some form of regular communication for informal check in times that best work for you and the employee. Check in can be done by a phone call or simply sending an email. This will help both of you stay on track and allows you to report any feedback that needs to be addressed. Think of it as keeping a close eye on your flock and ensuring that you are there for them if they happen to go astray.

Example forms of check in methods:

- Email
- Phone call
- Recurring group meeting
- Video chat

Remove Them

Sometimes after a manager has tried several attempts to help an employee work well on a virtual team, they come to realize that the particular employee is just not a great fit and will need to be removed. Some employees can be too disruptive to their teammates or are not able to work independently. This can cause problems for the whole team and should be addressed right away. Before you decide to remove the employee, make sure your ducks are in a row and that you have done all you can to help them succeed, such as personal help or extra training. If you have followed all of the correct guidelines and the employee does not show any type of improvement, then you can take the next steps in removing the employee from the virtual team. Some employees may be reassigned to another department in the company while others may need to be fired altogether. Review all of their available options and determine which would be best for the company and the virtual team.

Practical Illustration

Bridget was reviewing an employee's recent evaluation. Shannon was having trouble meeting her sales quota by the end of the month and hadn't contacted Bridget for any help. Bridget wondered what her routine was like since her end results were not coming out very well. Bridget decided to give Shannon a call at her office across town and discuss what was going on. When Shannon came on the line, Bridget asked her if she was having any problems or if she needed any assistance with her work. Shannon told her she was having trouble meeting her sales quota but hadn't put much thought into it. So Bridget decided to sign Shannon on for additional training with another lead member and hopefully boost some of her sales. She warned Shannon that if she did not put more effort into her work, she could be removed from the team and reassigned to another position.

Identify your problems but give your power and energy to solutions.

Tim Robbins

Chapter Ten: Choosing the Right Tools

Success on any kind of team depends on the tools you use to make it work. After all, you can't build a house without a hammer and you can't change a tire without a jack. But having a lot of tools at your disposal does not necessarily mean you have the right ones to get the job done. The key is in knowing what you want to do and what kind of tool would help you do it.

Communication Software

On a virtual team, communication software is crucial to have and use well. Employees are far apart and cannot communicate in person with each other when they have questions. How do your employees want or need to communicate with each other? For quick and easy questions or comments, text messaging or an instant message program can be the key. But if an employee needs to ask lengthy questions to a coworker or manager, a phone call or tagged email may be the answer instead. Whichever ways the team chooses to communicate with each other, it is just as important to know how to use and work the software, so be sure to ensure every employee has proper training and can come to you with questions.

Examples of communication software:

- Telephones – landlines, cellular or VOIP

- Email systems (AOL, Yahoo!, Gmail, Microsoft Outlook)

- Instant messaging programs (AOL IM, GroupWise Messenger, MSN messenger)

- Video chat room (Skype, ooVoo, Google Voice)

Collaboration and Sharing Tools

Collaboration and sharing tools allow team members across a virtual team to not only share a project they are working on, but also to work with each other by editing and commenting on projects within the same program. It can be a hassle to try and email a project back and forth when one person is trying to suggest a change or add their notes. There are a number of software programs that can be added to the virtual team to help make the collaboration process go more smoothly among team members. Many of these tools allow employees to upload a file for several others to see at once. Others include comment or adjustment features and can save any progress made after each person touches the file. These types of tools can make a virtual team run better and allows them to work as a team rather than several individuals trying to reach the same goal.

Examples of collaboration and sharing tools:

- Adobe Acrobat
- JotSpot
- Microsoft Office
- Novell GroupWise email
- Basecamp

Project Management Software

Project management software is aimed at managing the different aspects of a project, such as budgets, productivity, scheduling, communication, and even employee evaluations. There are many different ways of keeping track of this information, and companies normally take a different approach depending on the situation. Virtual teams generally have some sort of web based management program, such as web application for clocking in and out or keeping track of employee absences.

Other software options can include a program installed on the employee's desktop that can monitor their progress over a period of time and can show the employee what kind of progress they are making. Although we don't want to feel as though we are micromanaging our employees, it is necessary to implement some form of project management software for the team to use. While some may not like the approach to managing their projects, they will feel relieved when the time comes that they will need your feedback and guidance.

Use What Works for You and Your Team

Every manager has an opinion about what methods work and which ones do not for a virtual team. But only you can decide what works for you and your team. You know your employees and you know what would be the best way to communicate with them when you need to. Sometimes this can take some trial and error to see what forms of communication work best for the team as a whole. Some may communicate better by email while others are more comfortable talking on the phone. Many employees communicate using a number of different methods, depending on what kind of response they will need. The best part about having so many tools at your disposal is that you can use a combination of them to achieve what you and your team need to do.

Use the method, or methods, that get(s) what you need:

- Email/text messaging/phone calls – short answers and quick information delivery, such as a meeting change or a quick clarification question.

- Group meetings/individual meetings/video chats – in-depth and lengthy information given; usually requires explanations or discussions from both sides. This includes discussion of employee progress, business reports, or company changes.

Practical Illustration

Ira was sending a file back and forth to several team members for review. She was becoming frustrated that she would have several different versions in her email inbox and would have to continuously resend the file to her employees. She decided to include all of her projects in a form of Microsoft Office, which allowed her to use programs such as PowerPoint and Excel to manage her files. It also allowed her to share one file and allow several people to see it at a time so that if they made any changes, it wouldn't have to keep being resent. Although they used the phone for many of their informal meetings, Ira preferred to use the instant message program and form a chat room when she needed to collaborate on a project or idea. Ira found that it worked best for her and that she could get more accomplished when she found better ways of getting in touch with her teammates.

In terms of getting the kids working together and motivating them, the teacher is the most important.

Bill Gates

Closing Thoughts

- **John Le Care:** A desk is a dangerous place from which to view the world.

- **Paul Hawken:** Good management is the art of making problems so interesting and their solutions so constructive that everyone wants to get to work and deal with them.

- **Thomas J. Watson, Jr.:** I believe the real difference between success and failure in a corporation can be very often traced to the question of how well the organization brings out the great energies and talents of its people.

- **Agha Hasan Abedi**: The conventional definition of management is getting work done through people, but real management is developing people through work.

- **Lee Iacocca:** Start with good people, lay out the rules, communicate with your employees, motivate them, and reward them. If you do all those things effectively, you can't miss.

Made in the USA
Middletown, DE
03 December 2017